The Face You Draw into Your Skin is Not Your Own

poems by

Tricia Crawford Coscia

Finishing Line Press
Georgetown, Kentucky

The Face You Draw into Your Skin is Not Your Own

Publisher: Leah Maines

Editor: Christen Kincaid

Cover Art: Original Ink Drawing by Terence Main. Tattoo by Chris Pincus,
        Revelation Studios. Photographed by Joseph Coscia, Jr.

Author Photo: Joseph Coscia, Jr.

Cover Design: Elizabeth Maines McCleavy

Printed in the USA on acid-free paper.
Order online: www.finishinglinepress.com
            also available on amazon.com

Author inquiries and mail orders:
Finishing Line Press
P. O. Box 1626
Georgetown, Kentucky 40324
U. S. A.

Table of Contents

To all endangered species, including humans.

I

Lou joins us for Sunday dinner without you; he tells us
you are dissolving, fading
from pale to transparent.

Penumbra

The committee meets by phone, but I'm sure
they can hear my house—the wrens outside,
the faucet leaks, dog barks and neighbor's anger,
my pulse and the sirens that kindle it. The meeting
is as distant to me as the far-off turnpike murmur.

Instead of listening, I am googling: How do shadows
appear in outer space? What happens to mice
if they eat bar soap? My colleagues on the line
can't see the tiny teeth marks edging the Fels Naphtha
like stitches around a quilt patch, the mouse

stumbling across my floor as he steals a morsel,
while the ancient cat watches from his frayed chair,
unmoved. His opaque eyes—the shadow of rising
morning on this earth, his old brain clouded
by the fumes of your suicide.

Among my unanswered questions is why you didn't
let him out before you closed the garage door. Did you
mean to take him to your tomb, like an eternal servant?
Once, you bragged about his hunting prowess;
how he shared his kill with all the neighbors.

Perhaps in afterlife he would feed you, bring you
to the watering, make you drink herbal tea and ginger ale
without ice, until you could rise and come back to us.
I was up all night after the mistake of asking
whether carbon monoxide poisoning is painful. I learned

much more than I needed to know. You should have failed,
in these days of emissions requirements, which explains why
the cat is still with us, but you are not. It was all a mistake.
You only wanted to show us the depth of the darkness
but you fell inside it, left a shadow without a name,

a son without his mother, and a cat with eyes that blaze

the way the earth glows from behind the moon
as it passes during a lunar eclipse —
dark, red, wet, newborn.

She Imagines Herself Breathing

Perhaps she remembers a cedar shingle.
A splinter. A brick. How their mother painted
their soles and let them make footprints.
The currants, the blueberries, the woods.

Her grandfather's gardening stool, near
the swing-set where she hung by her knees
and upside-down sang the Dawning
of the Age of Aquarius. She notices

her sisters remember the whole house.
They visit it often. She only cracks
the blue door, taps the iron knocker. Inside
she might find kittens unfurling

under the bed, Mother-in-Law's Tongue
impaled hand-thrown pots, Spiderettes
dripping from macramé ropes, a doll
with hair shorn to nubs.

The gingham room. The canopy bed. A conch shell
whispers in her right ear. Thick fingers irritate
her shoulder blades, her collar bone, hot breath
in her left ear. She imagines herself breathing

through a marsh reed, burrowed in salt-mud.

Family Secrets

...the first appearance deceives many...
Phaedrus

The lavender-haired woman practices
with tall walking sticks as she imagines

climbing Everest in extravagant shoes
(sumptuous violet platform espadrilles).

The braided poet pries her roadkill
from a highway curbside, for the rough hide

and bones of her next bluegrass turnaround.
The brother is thinking of Quantum Theory

while picking a twelve string—does the love outside
who lotions their skin to a shine, hear him?

Lycra guilds their sturdy thighs, hair wild,
they sing the back-beats; the cousin composes

high, while selling wholesale office furniture.
One sister watercolors cats, the younger

smokes and plants coral begonias, a third
measures and pieces cotton mosaics.

While they whisper anxious histories
of nervous breakdowns, the oldest battles

a warehouse fire, her wife in Pima sheets
mouths a dream of flying, untouchable.

Each of them has ruminated how
to suicide, in a way that no one would know

what went on inside. Nor will anyone know
what compelled them to stay.

The Face You Draw into Your Skin is Not Your Own

As he scratches the blue-black
bird in my collarbone, he confesses;

he never goes anywhere
without telling his mother.

I hold questions in my throat.
He peels, like a stocking,

spattered latex from his hand.
A name peeks from his knuckles,

before he pulls on a fresh glove,
snaps it tight to his wrist,

unwraps the next needle. Pinches
the swallows' landing branches

across an age-spot, under a scar.
Strings vines across my clavicle.

Bogs the leaves in mint-green, olive
and indigo. The sting sets in.

We clear our throats.
I tell him why each swallow counts.

He tells me of a lost brother, etches
his mother's fear in the foraging

birds on my shoulder blade, scrapes
her wail into the scarlet and gold

weeds from which they tear their nest.
Washes the plasma buds from my scapula,

and leaves me with her haunted vigilance,
inked in the swallows' ready wings.

II

I see a spectacular collapse, disaster film,
slow motion, we witness every frame.
A volcano is roiling,

you are the trees caught in its wake, singed, prone.
Green life clings inside your branches.

Is this How it Starts?

One turn from the herd. An anvil cloud.

The compulsion of the mouse who can't stop
running in the wheel. It wears a ditch in the cedar chips. Leaves
its grass pellets in the dish, untouched. Quick lick
of the ball-bearing at the tip of the waterspout,
and it returns to the wire treadmill. It runs all night, oblivious
to sundown and cat-swats at the tank walls.

We no longer hear the wheel squeak, the mouse squeal, just as we
no longer notice maple leaves, the broken
sidewalk, potholes. Roadkill.

Our wheel is the bridge across the river. The road to our children
grows as they stay away longer. Our wheel is the path
to the back gate, to find you painting and sanding in the barn,
behind the kudzu we give up on in June. The mummified
fence. The trail of sticky bowls from refrigerator to stove

when everyone's home
and five dogs chase the yard.

Our wheel is the hall of damp towels and dusty books, steps that climb
to the bed that birthed a family who, even as adults, want
to sleep like puppies in a den. We cycle through our days and end
with the evening news. The tragedies multiply
outside. We know someone who knows someone
killed in a mass shooting. We know someone who died unarmed
at the hands of police. We know a few who've taken
their own lives. The same question keeps circling back:

What would we have done, if the eye was turned on us?

Massa

*The juvenile period for gorillas
is from three to six years and is characterized
by a decrease in maternal grooming, no longer sharing
a sleeping nest with the mother, and weaning.*[i]

I am twelve and conspicuously plain in the rare mammal house. I linger, check
my reflection in the dark glass of the sad cages: the limp feathered wings
of my Farah Fawcett haircut, lopsided breast-buds nudging
the purple stripe across my itchy Fair Isle sweater.

My family is watching the chimpanzees throw shit at one another; I pretend
I don't know them. I read the labels. I search for orphaned lowland Massa,
whose mother was shot as she foraged crops. This is how
Massa came to this zoo, where my awkward footsteps resonate
in clunky, fake-Frye leatherette boots:

*Almost all living primates have prehensile hands
and feet, and most have five digits on these
appendages, including opposable thumbs…
The hands are particularly sensitive, adding to the sense
of touch.*[ii]

From the death-colored tiles of his lonesome final habitat, everything echoes.
Massa rushes to the glass. We stare into one another's front-facing eyes.
He slouches over his Tastycake paunch; I lean toward him; the cold metal
snap of my hip-huggers probes my belly button. I lift my heels; press
my hand to meet his

against the glass, opposable thumb to opposable
thumb, nimble digits to nimble digits. We could be cousins, conspire
in his nest, point at the humans outside. I'd smudge
his rice sack with mascara tears, leave
on his neck a faint scent of Coty Musk, sooth
his cracked lips with bubblegum-flavored Bonne Bell.

Massa waves a wretched branch and wanders back through the dirty hay, past his tire swing to a dark corner. My mother pulls back my shoulder, sniffs. Did you use the Secret? Don't slouch, you look like Aunt Audrey. Are you wearing a bra? Your father was looking all over for you.

Female gorillas have been observed
to carry the bodies of their deceased infants
for weeks, even mating, while carrying a leathered corpse.[iii]

Secret Weapons

1981

We drive in Rita's green Pinto to the clinic,
every six months, pee in plastic cuplets, try not
to smudge our names before we slide our samples
through the mini door— snap it shut to alert
the lilac robed tech who collects our drips
and releases them on paper strips
like tiny paint store swatches.
She watches for their colors
to change, while we scan
glossy *Cosmo's*

and make fun of *Glamour* out loud,
although covertly, we slip the weight-loss tips
under our tongues. The waiting room is painted mauve.
Rita calls it pussy pink, wonders why the doctors can't get enough
of the shade. We laugh until our names are called; one of us cranks
the breast-exam view-master, hunts for lumps in fast-motion.
The other strips, redresses in paper thin as the sky, covers
white lies with small talk, pretending she is not
splayed open, her shame shielded by nothing
but a vinyl curtain, blush-cheeked despite
having read *Our Bodies/Ourselves*
from her mother's nightstand.

We leave with our treasure sacks
stuffed with six pink shells that open
to stiff viscera arranged like the clock,
little pills ticking inside. Buckle them in
our army surplus backpacks. It will be
another year or two before
we realize—even this
won't protect us.

2016

We knew what to expect
before we expected anything,
read *Whole Child/Whole Parent*, sealed
every outlet before we risked bringing anyone
into our uncertain world. For our daughters'
third and fourth birthdays, along with tutus
and matching magic glitter wands—
we gave them princess-pretty words:
Aureole, Labia, Clitoris, unleashed
for them to sing with abandon
as they rode fierce and fast
on berry colored bikes
and always

wearing their helmets.
As their breasts came into bud,
we introduced them to our fears
disguised with royal names—Chlamydia
Gonorrhea and Papilloma; shielded them
with Gardasil and coin purses full of Trojans.
Today our daughters hang their ankles
with confidence in the metal stirrups,
behind the curtains, barely wincing
as the midwife implants them
with tiny pickaxe babies,

to foil every seed, for the duration
of the presidential term. They don't cry
when their Achilles scrape, as they pull their feet
from the cold steel stirrups. Each womb bears
a warrior daughter: Para, Mirena, Liletta,
and Sklya[iv] wait in the quivers,
to sterilize lovers' quarrels
while the mothers
prepare.

Rules of Engagement for Combat Robots

Take time for your relationship to grow.
>Don't go galloping off to the minefield;
>stop and look, into one another's lenses.
>You will see yourselves reflected.

Use I language.
>Instead of, *Put down your weapon*
>*or I'll shoot,* try, *I need you to stop*
>*pointing your weapon at me.*
>*It makes me feel that I have to shoot you.*

Stick to the behavior, not the robot.
>Remember that she was programmed
>to plant that IED, just as you were
>taught to remove it.

Lean on your extended families.
>Let your elders prepare soft beds
>of lavender for your marriage, to grow
>through your engagement.

Learn from them but cultivate your own fields.

>Watch their tiller's spiked wheels plow
>through knotted grass roots, spitting
>rocks and flowerpot shards that sting
>limbs and tear eyes, like marriage fights.

>This may remind them of doors slammed,
>a hairbrush thrown across the room, but now
>sweat rivulets like amniotic fluids run
>down their clay-glazed, spider-veined calves,

>watering the soil they loosen, to allow
>root spread and easy growth. They wish
>just enough rain and sun, for you.

Lavender is hardy; the tiller is tough.

You will know better than they did, when not to shoot.

III

You reach for us, while you address
spirits at the foot of your bed.

The Understory

A raptor is living in our understory.
It spattered the windshield overnight
with milky blotches, frightened me into calling you
away from the kitchen, where you watched another breaking
moment, and said, like one of us does every night now,

See, this is where it all begins.
The pink Velcro sneaker dropped in the desert,
the poem on the kindergarten wall,
Lockdown, lockdown. Lock the door.
Shut the lights off. Say no more.[v]
A bag of shredded names.

Prey shrieks in the pachysandra. The raptor drops,
rises with a full beak through the magnolia umbrella.
Other creatures we can't see buzz in its wake, and on the porch,
the heavy transplant shovel falls over without being touched,
startling us both back inside. Another ICE raid on the screen

on our kitchen counter, every day screams
another rock-bottom.

Pool Hopping

A childhood friend replies to a Facebook post, 2016: *The great thing about this country is we are free to do as we please but if you block the road I want to drive down I will run you over if you try to stop me from voting I will take you out! If you try to move into my house without being invited, you will be DEAD.*

1976

Fourteen and free to do as we pleased,
we hopped fences (they were shorter, then).
When deck lights lit, we ducked
in arborvitae shadows,
hid behind boxwoods neatly cubed
by landscape crews, hired "for a song!"

Remember? We dipped in pools that glowed
in the dark, until their owners —
golfed, tanned, silky-robed and cock
tailed, razed us with flashlights. Even
as we ran away, their lawns cradled
our smug, bare soles, soft as plush.

      The unsent reply: *I have no need to keep you from the barren road
you tear in your shiny F150, nor to visit your granite kitchen, your garage
full of recreational vehicles. I'll stay in the softening barn, rouge
my cheeks with bicycle rust, drum a slat from the toboggan we crashed
on Robinhood Road, honor Grandpas wooden crates, the colors
of leftover paint. Let's just remember where it all came from.
Even the baby food jars, filled with nails, rusty and shiny,
smell like blood.*

2016

Memorize this, before we get too old —
Those lucky nights
when Mr. Smith and his flashlight
went back to bed,
we lay in clovery grass, not touching,

but side by side, Levi's and t-shirts
dew-damp. Glassy-eyed, Pop Rocks
buzzing our tongues, we marveled
at stars behind fireflies; how insignificant
we were.

When a boy runs across your driveway, forget
your legally-purchased handgun, leave it
with your fear, in its locked childproof cabinet.
Let him swim in your pool; watch him lay easy
on your lawn, savoring the Skittles on his tongue
while he stargazes and imagines
his infinity.

Thakil

Appear weak when you are strong, and strong when you are weak.
Sun Tzu, *The Art of War*

The father taking pictures knows that loss
decomposes. Like his child's skin gone to soil,

it regenerates, fuels his calves, he walks
and walks, flavors his eyes, he sees and shoots,

ignites his heart, it grinds on like the gears
in his photographs of orderly things.

It flakes from his son's painted tarps, the blacklined
figures that carry the weak

in fields where viruses multiply. He
replaces his son's wet brush and canvas

with a cold lens, resumes the contrast,
the harmonized patterns, restores the order

that fell like the green plum, before the yellow,
when the white haired one was left

to see off the black haired.

IV

Every time you die, I wake up hungry
from a dream, or is it a memory?
One of you sings Somewhere
Over the Rainbow. Some of us, eat peach pie.

If We Were There, There Would Be Colors to Remember.

You've captured the color I imagine the desert glows. Brittle gold, not
golden. Newspaper crackles in the back of an old frame, glass shards stuck
in the corners. Everything under the eaves. Pee shamed sheets under
our child's bed. What will it look like, when it's our turn to cross
a border? The basement wall, where this morning I emptied
the dehumidifier, and I wondered about the corners of our house
where we could hide people, if it ever comes to that.

I see the older wars in black and white, up to Vietnam. It came
home to us, on the small t.v. in the corner of the den, in the pages
of *Time*. I see the bomb drills in pea green, the shade of the cinderblock
walls where we knelt with our arms wrapped around our heads.
I cried through the first one.

After the bomb drill, the art teacher led me away from the wall, gave
me manila paper and crayons. The paper's undertone warmed the skies, the
grass and the blank rectangles of windows and doors, as if the sun shone from
the inside out. I drew a tree with long brown branches and green leaves—the
woods were my hiding place. I filled the tree with blood-red apples.

You color everything as if the sun is going down, if you use any color
at all. Our parents said, if you keep crossing your eyes, they will stay like that.
If you keep seeing things a certain way, will your vision stay like that?

If we were on-site at the front lines or at a border
crossing, there would be raw color to remember.

A silver blanket,

a purple sneaker,

a bruise.

Don't Un-see Her Eyes

Unseal your house on the first warm day;

read the fingerprinted panes. Write your name
in the sooted sill, count the frayed
rope-threads, test the loose sash. On the check rail's
brass latch, nests a candy egg, unfound,
since last Easter Sunday, wrapped in thin pink foil
as if to keep her warm until the hatch.

See how she foiled the ants, foiled summer, foiled melt.

foiled the children with their grassy, greedy baskets
and countless rides up and down the failing
window frame, that leaks cold drafts and lightning.
Her foil wrap incubates her, holds an inch
of sun-ray against frost. Your bloodshot eyes
echo in the mottled

pane. Recall how your son once believed

his basket of jelly beans and hollow rabbits
was a gift from a giant who trusted his virtue,
that fallen teeth yield gold coins under the pillow
and chimneys open wide to magically fit
a jolly fat man bearing brand new bicycles
and plastic houses. Your child slept clutching a ragged bunny.

He sleeps now like a venetian blind, eyes half open,

beside the radiator puffing warmth through the open window's chill
Try not to think of the photograph you saw,
the rubble matted fur in the clutch of another child
wrapped in a thin foil blanket, on an insufficient bed.
She thinks her mother is just down the road
they didn't tell her, when they lifted her from the wreckage…

Don't un-see her eyes, full of glass.

Pookie

The paper names you Young Black Male.
We don't know it is you, until

Addy hears it from one of your classmates. We remember
you, first in the kindergarten line every morning,

a warbling pot of finger-paint, waking us
with your whirling rhymes, your trampoline feet

and a knock-knock joke. You couldn't wait
for the principal to open the door. Your eyes romped,

your legs chuckled, and you squirmed
as your mother cupped your cheeks.

Addy says you died unarmed

running from the police. They kept your body for days
before they told your mother. I see your braids

wriggle from her fingers;
I see you crossing the finish line,

your knees embroidered with grass blades.
All the kids on the yellow team

want you to sign their shirts
and they shout your name,

Orenthia,

but you want them to call you Pookie.

V

I am making breakfast when
the phone rings.
I pry the pit from an avocado
with a dull, surgical-steel blade.

I bought the knife
because someone tried so hard
to sell it. (You understood.)
The pit pops from the belly, spins

on the counter like roulette,
slows, stops
dead on the edge without falling.

Reliquaries—Aunt Anna Babysits

Hail Mary, full of grace

Aunt Anna on her knees
prays her fifty-three
Hail Mary's, our morning shield.
I am the eavesdropper, counting down. Pious
spy anointed secret lookout.
She prays for us sinners,
pours her heart in her hands. Quivering
fingers

the Lord is with thee,

explore the rosary.
She eyes her shrine,
Infant of Prague in plastic shroud,
crisp purple vestment, shiny world in His hands.
His eyes behold His adult self
crucified, tarnished
nightstand relic, perpetual
fraught gaze.

blessed art though among women and blessed

Down the hall, Cousin Grace
opens the crawl space,
arranges her reliquary,
contraband lipstick, lighter, condoms, weed.
Time left to steal two cigarettes
and seven dollars
from Anna's cloth purse. We urchins
covet.

is the fruit of thy womb

Anna beseeches plastic St. Francis,
heart cleft and dying
of sweetness, broken blessing hand,
*Guide us through the furnace of love—Children
are mysteries.* She says beneath
his blistered cassock
he holds for us a secret nectar—

———

Jesus. Holy Mary, Mother of God

Hail Mary's winding down
rosary complete.
Blessed am I and my cousin,
everyone we've lost, the world without end.
Anna feeds us, takes us to school.
If she knows our sins
she doesn't hold them against us,
again.

Pray for us sinners

Cousin Grace, ten years hence,
queen of the disco
universe, blue sequin jumpsuit
silver Maximillian around her neck,
grief without end, strung out, comes home
for Anna's solace
as it was in the beginning
amen.

VI

You should see this—the flea-market clutter,
in the meeting house social room
covered with sheets, out of respect
for your memorial service.

There are No Stupid Answers

Stupid hisses across the room,
follows you home into bed before
sundown, dumbfound, untied shoes
on a thumb-sucking girl hiding
in the linens.

Stupid drops a fork, screeches
a knife on porcelain, breaks a Lenox
teacup and drops a silver-plated tray
with all her thumbs.

She is too busy reading dust motes,
spellbound by the hues that seep through
closed eyelids. Stupid rumors,
the sledge in hammer. Stupid can't
understand our language. Stupid

doesn't talk right. Stupid line-dances
in the wrong direction. Stupid
can't do Origami, doesn't understand
Business Casual; Stupid won't lie

to protect herself. Stupid should try
therapy. But no one will believe her
anyway. Stupid misses the instructions
while staring at the floor. Stupid
should not have opened that door, Stupid

should learn to say *no*. She should learn to say
I know. But Stupid learns to keep secrets.

VII

It looks like a morgue in here. The Protestant's clock across the pond, awkwardly chimes noon, at ten a.m..

Sidewalk Ghosts

For a moment, you hear the trickle of water
through icy rocks, and remember the paths
created by child-steps, headed to the creek to gig frogs,
by old men with gnarled walking sticks and binoculars,
searching the trees for rare birds, mothers

in aprons calling us home. The paths wound
past landmarks—tire swing, broken dam, lady's
slipper. Raspberry prickers grazed naked legs in summer
slugs melted between our toes after the rain. Now frozen
boot-prints, in terracotta gravel, evenly backhoed,

recall our feet in thin plastic sandwich bags, the twist
of the Flexible Flyer to avoid a scrape with paled
and brittle brush. Sodden mittens, snow on pachysandra, steamy
breaths before the trip back up the hill. Cigarette
cellophane crackles underfoot,

cans overflow a recycling bin along the curb, in front
of Hooper's Funeral Home, where electric candles burn
in the windows, even in midday. A man walks by—
his leather fedora and Members Only jacket
reminds you of Charlie,

who first kissed his wife behind the old leaf dump
and Jen, whose Christmas wreath still hangs on her door. The silence
leaves room to imagine: Chris's Harley up the drive at 3 a.m.,
Jesse wrestling his brother at the Halloween party, dressed
in his mother's nightgown,

the poetry of the different-hat-each-day man, spoken only
to telephone poles. His presence you assumed;
his absence,
no one else seems to have noticed.

On the Road to St. Mary's

Morning opens across the reservoir—
stretches somber limbs, winterizing sky
lights a doe carcass iced, mired in pasture,
fur draped like a matador's cape, blood dyed,

sequined with mirror shards, shredded rubber
farm stubble beaded with windshield and ice,
homespun cross rises in flowers, anchors
ragged wool bunny with acrylic eyes.

Just down the road my mother refuses
one last procedure, she won't be confined
in her own body, pulsing and alive
while her mind creeps away from her and dies.

Morning evaporates as we drive home; a road crew dispensed
with the carcass and shrine.

My mother says, when you stop making memories, there is nothing
left but this time.

VIII

You'd have noticed; remember that Sunday?
You stood and stopped
the mantle clock's incessant ticking.

That's How it Goes

I believe you, when you say there are deer in the photograph, even
though you've obscured them. I hope they are far from the tracks—I remember
that winter, riding home from the city. The kids still believed in Santa; distance
glittered with Christmas. The clatter of antlers under our feet, a buck caught
by the train. The drinking man across the aisle joked about Rudolf,
how he went from Christmas celebrity to nothing, just like that.

"That's how it goes," he said.

Like the mice that litter the corners of our pantry, finished in a snap.
I found another nest they left behind, in the low cabinet that holds the spoils
of birthday parties and holiday crafts—glow-in-the-dark lanyard, crepe paper,
Modge-Podge and soap molds. Nothing for a mouse to eat, but plenty in which
to make a bed.

The thick sprinkle of their droppings could be mistaken for bugle
beads or chocolate jimmies, scattered across the calico shelf liner. It smells
like animal sex—too strong for two little mice. They've had an orgy
in the pantry. In the pastel tissue papers, beneath a gift bag strung
with ribbon threads, a last wild festival before we caught them
one by one and dropped them in their plastic coffins. They traded their lives
for a lick of peanut butter.

This morning a deer lay still in the bypass, neck curved back, eyes
open, as if she were giving one last glare to the absurd highway
that splits the forest.

Imprimatura

Piss on the chicken's corn
and they will lay healthy.

Cast an egg on the gravel near
where your enemy draws water
and he will go away.

Cast one on the east wall
every day for nine days
and the affair will end,
although you will still have egg
on your house.

Fall asleep in your clothes
watching a PBS special
on the Shroud of Turin
and wake up remembering
you forgot to dye the eggs.

Google why you do this
and learn that these things
are related. The cracked shell,
an open tomb. Red dye,
the blood left behind.

For a hint of biblical authenticity,
use onion skins and muslin.
Cage-free brown eggs, for natural
imprimatura, a golden
undertone (and no harm done).

When dyed, their hues are deep
sapphire against darkest forest
soil, lily pollen on fire,
violet heavy in night shadow
during the blood moon, ruby,

rust of war. While preparing
the dye, you learn that the thoughtful
boy from your Sunday school
is going back to Iraq. You leave

in its plastic wrapper, the tablet
that would fizz into crimson.

This Picture Will be Hard to See, but Look at it Anyway

Hunker down with the ravaged nurses
of these five untimely babies

on the broken Aleppo pavement,
disconnected from incubators,

sucking air through rubble-crusted lips.
wrapped in flannel mantels, fading,

The torn building there, in the distance,
ruin of the hospital that held them,

the nurses forced to lift each one
from their warm cocoon, and unfasten

the tubes that beat their premature hearts.
That is where our ordnance landed.

Nearby, their mothers and fathers lie buried—
the babies did not make themselves up.

Before, they had brothers and sisters
who played hide-and-seek in jasmine gardens

outside unbroken homes, like you once did.
When you see this, you will pray—you will yearn

to believe they survived, and you might go
without Novocain, imagining

as the dentist drills a nerve, how one might grow
her baby teeth, only to have them knocked

asunder, before they have time to loosen
themselves. You will think of this photograph;

knowing, odds are, one of them will take shrapnel
in his belly within the year, if he lives to see it.

You will want them to rise from their swaddles,
and walk outside your nightmares.

Relics

Lucy phones and knits, clicking
needles as we talk of sons,
unraveled from our spheres.
She drops a stitch and curses war
darns a hole while we inventory
the gifts of earlier Mothers' Days:

- plaster handprints, bejeweled
- tongue depressor boxes of foraged
- feathers and beachcombed
- fortunes, grass blades, captured caterpillar,
- jar lid on which he bloodied
- his hand, breath holes hammered
- in hopes of metamorphosis

Her son has come home and left
again. He leaves footlockers
stacked to her shoulders, dark
as the underside of roadside snow.
As we talk, she opens the lockers
for a glimpse of what he's carried home:

- battle helmet lined with bullet-stopping
- maze; walk-about helmet,
- lined with nothing, mother-
- of-pearl-handled gun, tight-woven
- scarves of many colors, once drawn
- over quivering chins, under night goggles,
- while dodging roadside IEDs. Afghan sand spills

everywhere, it grouts her Pergo floors
grits the yarn from which she knits him
a desert-shaded winter scarf, nubbed
to remind him of the places they traveled
together, and the small treasures
he once collected:

- Chincoteague sand dusting warped
- pine floorboards, his little suitcase
- packed to the gunwales, sand spitting
- whirligigs and kites, bursting
- from cartoon-charactered
- swim trunk seams, balled-up
- socks and pocketed rocks,

and later, his spring break
bounty—Cozumel sand, mortaring
crevasses of a hammered metal gecko,
weighting a rip-stop nylon back-pack,
one sand-dollar to his name.
As she reminisces:

- my son comes home from sledding
- pink faced, breathless,
- sweat-frozen scarf, rock-salt crusted
- slush and road sand dribbles
- from his snow boots, disappears
- into the floor.

IX

*The waterfall responds to construction
by damming itself; a slow muddy trickle
reflects new aluminum townhouses
in your neighborhood.*

The Club at Landfill Lake

The landfill mountains have doubled in size
since her birth, we wonder—how high will they grow?
This could be Darjeeling foothills, undulating

green and breathing. Ella says *It's just that morning*
makes it look that way, when the air is still clear
and the sun polishes the lake. We expect yaks

on steppes, but these foothills attract only rats
and gulls, and the fish in the water are bleaching,
slow and cloud-eyed. Between the train tracks

and the manmade lake, cabins line up, their private
garbage pits seething. We partied here, one 4th of July,
peed in a trailer loaded with bottle rockets and M80's.

Chris, between cancers, launched potatoes into the lake,
just in front of a line of swimming geese, he'd aim
to reverse their course, then splash one on the other side

and they turned again, and we laughed again. But Chris
didn't turn around that time. The signs everywhere,
say *you must belong*, and unwritten signs say *you must*

be white. But nothing warns of the poison steeping,
the methane exhaled from PVC sprouts. No Kelsang,

no prayers strung from Sherpa shacks, no bright weavings

here. Our colors burst and turn to ash.

Erasure

A day blushes between trestle arches
above the rusted river. Flickering
leaves like fishes tempt, the Great Blue Herons
stab and vanish into pinking fog.

I'd like to stop and frame it just like this,
but the road offers no shoulder, no path
beside the shifty flood-withered bank.
My attention turns to the yellow lines;

a garbage truck lurches and masticates
the remains of our neighborhood bounty.
Styrofoam, chicken bones and bendy straws,
rickety fill for our bulldozed mountains.

I think about the original ones,
their hunts and gardens, shared shelters of elm
and hide, rush beds, when this land was beyond
the edge of Yong's wilderness, long before

we built bridges to bring them our burdens,
baked the red clay pulled from their riverbed
into strip malls, minced timber to pressboard
walls for locked-door master bedroom suites.

Their watertight baskets are afterthoughts
on the shelf behind musket balls and fifes
in the local historical museum
where every year, two weeks before Christmas,

"George Washington" pulls up on an old horse.
Fist buttoned in his mother's white glove,
he knocks on the door below the bug-proof light,
bows to this year's acting Mrs. Barclay,

and asks, although the audience knows the answer,
May we occupy your land?

Ignore the Expiration Date

Viewed without my glasses, the bog surface imitates our back stoop—littered
with smashed wild cherries, painted with pastel bird droppings, the dog's
clipped fur. The dandelion that grows from a crack, a bitter salad,
but good for the kidneys, and costs us nothing. My mind goes home.

As the money tightens, we learn to forage and groom
our own dogs. One has grown so sturdy, so lush
we could mop the floor with her. She spins in circles
in the yard, pees on our greens. Last night I was upset

at all the food we throw away. Mad at the big dog for stealing
a burger. Mad at the rabbits who murder a salad every day
in the garden. Mad at the piss on our future harvest. The bog,
like our garden, glows in its decay. And now I see what I am looking at—

the salt marsh seething its way back, eating the cedars and sycamores
from the roots up, choking the needles and leaves. As the earth fights back,
we will relearn our gleaning. Let the bees live. Pull the invasive species
by their roots, redefine weeds, let the pokeweed and dandelion flourish.

Ignore the expiration date, and eat that can of beans we were saving
for the apocalypse.

X

*You'd hate the aesthetic. Someone else lives
in your stone and color houses. None of this
was supposed to happen. You were all
supposed to grow old with us.*

Spitting for Distance

Armed with a garden hose,
fitted with brass muzzle, spitting

fierce enough to splinter oak,
I amputate the gluey silk

Funnel Weaver has laced along
gutters and flashing, sash

and shutter, beneath the wind-chimes,
inside the lantern glass. I murder

what the spider has sculpted: her sticky
web-hands that nestle egg sacs and snag

her prey between spindle and cane;
her woven podia exposing

our debris—the mothy unswept porch,
Ella's spit seeds left to molder

and soot. Marked by my torrent, spider's
wooly eggs clutch a worn board,

a dry crevasse of brick stoop, before
the riptide abducts them curbside,

disappears them down the sewer grate.
Tegeneria Domestica

escapes the flood, sidles along
a broken umbrella spine, scuttles

over a mud-cake alphabet
shaken from our boots. She takes cover

in the rocking chair behind a curl
of peeling paint. Three furred legs reveal her.

I can see her, but she can't see me,
although that night I imagine her

glaring from her unraveled lair.
Fragments of her spawn soak

into our nightshirts from the hose-damp
cushions where my daughter and I gulp

the wet night, the waning summer
only visited. Ella cracks

seeds in her teeth, spits shells
in the Burning Bush. I scold her

for the misses that litter our porch,
blame her for the mice and other

infestations. She ignores me, spits
harder, gleeful for the distance

she achieves. Reloads, until she is out
of ammunition, and the mosquitoes,

unfettered by spider webs, force us
inside. Funnel Weaver, left to darn

her damaged snares, restrings the porch
with hammock traps, fills them with fresh

cotton eggs, while in our separate rooms
we scratch, press blood-clumped fingernails

to each round welt, etching x's to stop the itch,
marking our bites, as my mother taught me,
and I taught my daughter.

Joe-Pye, Fifth of July

Between the Joe-Pye and maple trees,
beach grasses shimmy finches
and monarchs from their slim pockets.
The forest shush, in flock they sway,
broom-whisking peasants disturbing
litter at their feet.

One stray brown loafer is flattened
beneath a shattered whiskey fifth,
too heavy for the gusts to lift.
Firefly roused from day-sleep rises
from the shoe, reminds me of you,
leaping the meadow,

circa seventy-nine, the one
who delighted in dress-up, pranks,
magic tricks and trash-picked sofas,
busting ghosts. Fireworks would not come
fast enough. Now your eyes have grown
to butterfly nets,

swill beauty and offer it back,
music from your sugar-cookie
tongue. Thin arms catch birds and let them
go in zephyrs. That heavy shoe
and broken bottle mean nothing,
just old reminders

of a party out of control.
The leather will decay and feed
the soil, the bottle will splinter
into glimmers on the dance floor
of the swaying grasses. Notice,
how long they have been

waltzing on only one foot
each, held up by one another.

Branches in the Swamp/ Roots in the Sky

Turn yourself upside down—see your branches as roots.
Imagine your roots as branches spread in the swamp
muck, harboring crayfish and tadpoles. The roots inhale
the sky. That is, if you are deciduous.

Red cedar, or hemlock needles would scratch
silver scales from the fish, glitter the bog. Upended
in the swamp, you drag your fingers like car wash sponges,
trapping water skates and frogs for a fresh meal.

If you are Holly, you'll be like thistle to a turtle's tender gums.

Are we evergreen, bent to gather what the current brings,
let it ornament our branches like battle scars
or do we shed our leaves and let the mud flow through,
bare our roots to the elements?

It would be easy to stand as a tree, cast
a silhouette in the moonrise over the landfill,
lay a shadow on the robin's-egg blue door
of the box store, shelter the daisy that rises through the gravel
sway above the grasses in the track swale, as the unsurvivable

Acela passes,
leaving a wake of gnat carcasses.

XI

Someday the living will don our hearing devices,
clatter our wheeled walkers into meeting
on Sunday, become the old ones repeating
stories of how you stopped the clocks.

It's as if You Met My Grandfather.

I see Kudzu blankets, daisy banks, big old stone walls, copious green
foliage outside my train. You text me the reflections, and the view outside
your window. The bridges that invade the marsh birds' flight paths, steel
webbed towers—transformers—what is it they transform?

You've caramelized the factories. Aged the image
so I might think you are Instagramming from 1960, yet you have made it
timeless, like rock walls and stout maples. Those steel towers have not
been around forever, and they throw no seed.

What if we could start again— babies, waving from twin carriages.
Go through our childhoods together, foraging acorns to make doll-size salad
bowls in the fairy garden, falling off bikes. Maybe you would have taught me
to ride, before I gave up trying. You would meet my grandfather,
taste his currants and jam. He'd teach us to weed, and tread carefully
at the edges of the marsh.

He could tell us what it looked like here. Before the bridges, the Kudzu,
the Devil's Walking Stick, and the transformers.

The Clay will be Our Salvation

The erosion under I-95 might surprise you.
The spring torrents left a wake of drink

cups, gravel and chrome bits. A giant
mound of red clay. If the road above were shelled

that clay would be our salvation, holding up
the cement slab above the train. Your sky

is mottled, mine is clear this morning. We ride
under the lines that pull us in opposite directions

yet at the source, the same power that takes us apart
pulls us back home. Under the clay is an aquifer—

its water reaches north, beneath the warehouse farms
and what's left of the marsh. It tongues the caverns

under your building. I bet it's beautiful, underground
lit by flashlight, where the climate never changes.

Nava Rasa—*Nine Emotions*

Abdutha
Sun-freckled, bare arm
curved like Nataraja. A chameleon
on her crooked elbow,
anti-freeze green, gaping at her.

Hasya
She gazes from the frame, amazed,
Tanzania in the background,
the laughter I remember
from across the kitchen table.

Karuna
Joy in her hand, outstretched
from the back door, feeding
crackers to the raccoons
so the birds will not go hungry.

Bheebhatsya
Her voice thickens
at the nightly news, Napalm,
Neo-Nazis, NRA. I inherited her
clenching teeth, tightening belly.

Raudra
My mother held fast
in a maple casket atop
my father's, tamped down
by the flag she questioned.

Bhayanaka
She rests on ivory silk,
the word for it would be
gossamer, but it is folded
thick as a hot-plate.

Veera
The prayers begin.
—Om mani padme hum—
incense coils over her
reflection in blue glass.

Shringara
I hear, Oh Mommy,
the March Ice Storm, she said
fairies strung diamonds on the trees
for my fifth birthday.

Shantha
Her spirit curls into the smoke
incense lingers like her coat
still holds scarlet lipstick,
and always a tissue in the pocket.

The scent of Shalimar stays in the wool,
the way her gaze lingered on all living beings.

Dogs are Something Most of us Can Agree On

The Monday after we created a wall of teddy bears and messages
on the congressman's fence, I woke up from a nap as the train was stopped
between two stone walls. I imagined The Wall built up block by block
by the hands of incarcerated immigrants. They are all muscle and callous,
palms thick enough to walk on. They will build it solid,
and build themselves out.

I imagine, in 28 years or so, tearing it down. A cheering crowd, a dented
brass band. Children who once lost their families are young adults. They help
their older parents take strikes at the wall with a sledgehammer. I want
to be the old one on the sidelines with a defiant smile, who remembers the day
we said, "History will not be kind." I try to be forgiving, but some things are
unforgivable. I pocket a handful of mortar dust to scatter on a grave.

We used to be the haven.

A great grandchild on my lap; I tell her about the survivors—
the exonerated prisoner and the murder victim's sister who fell
in love at the bus stop, the student who made it out of a school massacre
and is now our president, The woman who waved to us every day
from her porch across from boarded-up row homes, the community
garden down the street, tilled by neighbors of all faiths. Glass deer
and silk flowers in the window that faced the train tracks.

I tell her how every day we asked ourselves, "What can we do?" We
never had a clear answer, so we just did. Some went to jail, some took bullets
to protect others; one took rabies shots to his knee, so the dog that bit him
could live, because he couldn't imagine living without his own dog. I tell her
the dogs were the one thing we could all agree on.

XII

Nothing we say can improve the silence,
or render for us the fidgets and sighs
as one of you clenches a needle
between her teeth

one wriggles in place, willing for a sound,
another bends to feed the cat
and you take your place on your favorite bench,
second to last from the back, on the right.

The Soft Spot

My eyes, according to you, were weird.
      Large for a baby, newborn blue, they roamed

      over pimpled siblings' and cousins' faces,
when the parents brought me home. I wish

I could remember how you received me,
      passed the flannel bundle and tested

      my grip with your sticky fingers.
You said you fought for your turn,

traded your right to change the channel,
      for a chance to hold me longer,

      handing me over only for the Twilight Zone.
I conjure you there in the playroom

I remember best, the oily paint,
      plywood closet layered with tinker toys,

      snarled-hair dolls frayed in homemade dresses,
vinyl electric breath spinning

from the console. I slid its doors apart,
      poked the taut cloth that hid the speakers,

      sniffed and licked, when no one was looking,
its curved laminate ribs. I had a secret,

a gold finger
      that could feel the singer inside.

      If I peered into the sound I could see
a tiny tambourine man blowing in the wind.

The taste, like scotch sucked from parents' ice,
        crocheted afghans soaked in the smoke of pilfered

        Lucky Strikes, the magic dragon reek.
I survived your flying carpet rides,

the baby aspirin you fed me,
        playing doctor, the unraveling

        tire swing, the fall. I wish I could remind you
how you taught me to lie down and stare at an oak

from her base, roll my spine over her acorns.
        I wish I could tell you that no harm was done,

        when you thought no one was watching, and you
probed the soft spot on my newborn skull,

        waiting for it to vibrate like the stereo.

What is Wrought can be Undone

A bird does not sing because he has an answer. He sings because he has a song.
Joan Walsh Anglund

Bluebird houses like posted sentries tick the highway miles. In beige-edged
thicket, cellophane gleams and twines with Cheatgrass and Poverty Brome.
Wiley mockingbirds bed their nests of Weeping Lovegrass with tinsel fortunes
and old rubber bands.

This is the road that leads to my parents' cemetery. In winter we rested
my father; my mother just before spring, as the bluebirds returned. The sight
of one, today, like something taut un-sprung, calls up the day she taught me

the word *extinction,* ahead of her time in the fogged shelter of our four-doored
Chrysler, air vents shuttered, we waited for the DDT to finish its neighborhood
misting. The passenger-sidewindow offered a panorama of her warnings:

invasive Seven-Sisters, pale spotted petals, rashy leaves and sick-thorned
skeletons that pierced the palm who tried to release them from the strangling
Mile-a-Minute. The chrome of accidents, and lone shoes. Her generation knew

empty chairs and orphaned parents, trauma, although they had no words
for it. She'd abhorwhat we've become, sprayers of bees before they've stung,
arming our children before they've sung their alma-maters. Beyond

the kudzu-mummified wisteria, a man sits in a diner-themed kitchen,
surrounded by mannequins and semi-automatics, while next door a father
accidently sets an extra plate at the dinner table. We are willing

our own apocalypse, some to survive, others for permission to finally let go.
But something small, a dust mote in a parent's bedroom, tickling a mother's
eyelid, and any of us might not be here, or might be someone else

who didn't survive infection, pre-antibiotics, near starvation, the wayward
toddler parking-lot dash, and live to someday connect egg to sperm
and hold on long enough to birth me, or you, or the weapons collector

or the blue bird housemakers, who managed to save a species in time
for my mother to see one fly, and know that what she warned of was unsung.

You Might Have Read the Horoscope

The Lion has married the Fish,

one ruled by Jupiter, the other
governed by the Sun. Both felled
by Mercury, which rolls in retrograde

today, as the newlyweds deflate paper lanterns,
fold the party tents, anoint the pasture
with flat champagne. A half-drowned firefly
escapes. They toss the zinnias, once carefully

arranged, into compost for the worm bin,
the vases' clotted water feeds the trampled
grass where we stomped and clapped
all night. Now they unstring tiny lights,

lay their private constellations in the truck bed,
drive them home to grace my daughter's childhood
peeling porch, where the family gathers for farewells,
and you are missed. But your wary old cat,

spies through cataracts your son, who raised him
as a kitten. The cat lumbers on incoherent hips,
rubs thinning fur against the boy's familiar
legs, lengthened seven years since the mourning

of your last breath, when your son and his cat
were homed apart. You should see how
your boy's wrists and ankles sprout like branches
as he bends to scratch the ancient, coyote-scarred

bird watcher in his wicker throne. When he looks
at me, I see your glance behind the rose-blazoned
bow that graced your shoulder, years ago
on my wedding day, before my daughter and her groom,

or your son and the cat orbited in, before
your constellation read suicide, while ours spelled
survive. I see you holding a toddler, a kitten
in his lap, the world card turned over. I see him

yesterday in outgrown dress shoes, on the pew
beside his aunt, witnesses to the newlywed's elysian
gazes, reflecting the sun in Leo, the moon in Pisces.
They say Pisces travels in a veil of silver

while Leo soars in broad daylight, winged.
Tomorrow the moon will eclipse the sun;
all of us will watch the sky curl dark,
reveal the constellations, and unfold back to light.

End Notes

[i] Quoted from Cawthon Lang, KA. "Primate Factsheets: Gorilla (Gorilla) Behavior." Primate Info Net (2005). 20 May 2019. <http://pin.primate.wisc.edu/factsheets/entry/gorilla/behav>.

[ii] Kelly, Jasey. What are the Major Characteristics of Primates. ND. 20 May 2019. <http://animals.mom.me/major-characteristics-primates-3721.html>.

[iii] Quoted from Warren, Ymke and Williamson, Elizabeth A. Transport of dead infant mountain gorillas by mothers and unrelated females. 28 July 2004. Online Source. 20 May 2019. <http://onlinelibrary.wiley.com/doi/10.1002/zoo.20001/abstract>.

[iv] Para, Mirena, Liletta, and Sklya are the brand names of IUDs (Intra-Uterine Devices).

[v] Original quote source unnamed, from an article by Chiu, Allyson. "'Shut the lights off, say no more': Nursery rhyme prepares kindergartners for lockdowns." Washington Post (2018). <https://www.washingtonpost.com/news/morning-mix/wp/2018/06/08/lockdown-lockdown-is-a-kindergarten-nursery-rhyme-at-massachusetts-school/?utm_term=.83c885b32b48>.

Acknowledgements

Family and community made this possible, and teachers made the difference that makes it real. I am forever grateful to Young Smith, whose guidance, gifted sense of the connecting power of language, wisdom in craft, and patience inspired and steered my writing and thinking. Thanks to Skye Van Saun for teaching me to write bravely, Ethel Rackin for encouraging me to keep going, all the Bluegrass Writers Studio for creating a safe nest for experimentation, and to Carter Sickels for seeing the tangles in my drafts and offering thoughtful feedback. To my husband Joe for 30 years of support, love and the inspiration to write, and Linda Sepe, thank you for reading everything and for believing. Sue Whittaker, who reminded me that friendships transcend time and age, and whose faith and generosity found me when I needed it most. Thank you, Gracie, Addy, Ella and Sam, for guaranteeing an audience, and giving me reason for everything I do. I'm grateful to Finishing Line Press for seeing this collection as worth sharing and to Christen Kincaid, Leah Maines and Elizabeth Maines McCleavy for their help in seeing it through.

The poem "The Face You Draw into Your Skin is Not Your Own" was published in *Connecticut River Review,* August 2018. "Thakil", "Secret Weapons" and "Rules of Engagement for Combat Robots" were published in the anthology *50/50: Poems & Translations by Women Over 50,* Quills Edge Press, 2018. "Pool Hopping" was published in *Peregrine Journal,* 2018. A slightly different version of "Sidewalk Ghosts" was published in *Parting Gifts,* March Street Press, 2012. "Erasure" and "Pookie" appeared in *The Chaffin Journal.*

Young Smith helped me see the title in "The Face You Draw into Your Skin is Not Your Own" grapple with the order of the collection, and he provided the phrase "leathered corpse" in "Massa". The poem on the kindergarten wall that is quoted within "The Understory", *Lockdown, lockdown. Lock the door. Shut the lights off. Say no more,* is from Allyson Chiu's haunting article about how schools are addressing the specter of school shootings, " 'Shut the lights off, say no more': Nursery rhyme prepares kindergartners for lockdowns", Washington Post, June 8, 2018.

To my giant family, my dear ones here and gone, I write always with you in my heart. This collection would not exist without the people and other endangered species who inhabit and influence the poems—the empaths, brawlers, and gorillas, who offer occasions for love, and everything that goes along with it.

Tricia Crawford Coscia was born in Long Island, New York during a time when DDT rained from small planes in the summertime and girls were not allowed to wear pants to school. One of eight children, she was raised by multiple loving siblings as well as her parents, allowed to roam in the woods, and she had access to plenty of books and art supplies.

The Vietnam War and the struggle for civil rights entered their home through *Life* Magazine and the evening news, and the specter of the draft for her older brothers. Tricia witnessed the post war resilience of her grandparents, parents, aunts and uncles as well as her older siblings' resistance to norms as they entered adulthood during the Vietnam War. Her father had lingering scars having been a prisoner of war in World War II, and her mother bore the grief of her brother's death in the Battle of the Bulge. Her mother taught them to care for others and the land they inhabited, wary of insecticide and weed killer, fearless of snakes and lizards, a boycotter of grapes.

During her pre-adolescence, Tricia's family moved from Long Island to the Main Line outside Philadelphia, where extraordinary wealth and unquestionable privilege were the norm. Schools were not segregated by law but by human behavior. It was the 70's, and feminism was at an awkward early stage that meant sexual freedom but not agency—a difficult realm in which to navigate coming of age. The creative and open atmosphere of art school in the 80's became haunted by the AIDS epidemic and stigma around sexuality. Working for Art Against AIDS in the late 1980s, Tricia was impacted by the loss of so many of the artists she worked with who supported the campaign. She married photographer Joe Coscia, and together they built a life around family and art, raising four children, many pets, images and poems.

Joe and Tricia moved back to Pennsylvania to live closer to their aging parents and grow a garden. A visit to Quaker Meeting out of curiosity about Joe's ancestors led to their joining and raising their children as Quakers. Tricia worked as a caregiver in a multigenerational facility where her children could attend, at an alternative school, and a neighborhood social service resource center. Somewhere along the way she began writing poetry and participating in online workshops. At the Dodge Poetry fest, she met poet Skye Van Saun. Skye became an important mentor and teacher. Tricia formally studied writing at Bucks County Community College with Ethel Rackin, and later received her MFA in Creative Writing from the Bluegrass Writers Studio.

Currently, Tricia seeks to be more outspoken and courageous, to be a co-conspirator against racism and white supremacy, and to challenge complacency about the eroding environment through her personal experiences and imaginations. The exonerated death-row survivors she works for through

Witness to Innocence provide a model of courage and grace. She and her husband commute in opposite directions. She draws inspiration from his photographic conversations, the changing environment, dogs and other living beings, and raising children in an often adverse, economically and environmentally unjust, yet still beautiful world.

www.ingramcontent.com/pod-product-compliance
Lightning Source LLC
Chambersburg PA
CBHW021153090426
42740CB00008B/1074